Poems about the

Natural World

Evan Voboril

Raintree is an imprint of Capstone Global Library Limited, a company incorporated in England and Wales having its registered office at 7 Pilgrim Street, London, EC4V 6LB – Registered company number: 6695582

www.raintreepublishers.co.uk
myorders@raintreepublishers.co.uk

Produced for Raintree by White-Thomson Publishing
www.wtpub.co.uk
+44 (0)843 208 7460

Edited by Sonya Newland
Cover design by Tim Mayer
Designed by Alix Wood
Concept design by Alix Wood
Production by Victoria Fitzgerald
Originated by Capstone Global Library Ltd
Printed and bound in China

ISBN 978 1 4062 7290 1
17 16 15 14 13
10 9 8 7 6 5 4 3 2 1

British Library Cataloguing in Publication Data
A full catalogue record for this book is available from the British Library.

Poems reproduced by permission of:
p. 33 COLLECTED POEMS 1930-1986 by Richard Eberhart (1988) 48 lines "The Groundhog". By permission of Oxford University Press, USA, and in markets not controlled by OUP by the Richard Eberhart Estate.
p. 39 Dana Gioia, "Planting a Sequoia" from *The Gods of Winter*. Copyright © 1991 by Dana Gioia. Reprinted with the permission of The Permissions Company, Inc., on behalf of Graywolf Press, Minneapolis, Minnesota, www.graywolfpress.org and Dana Gioia.
p. 45 Nikki Giovanni, "The Yellow Jacket". Copyright © 2007. Reprinted by permission of the author.

Picture credits can be found on p. 63

CONTENTS

Experiencing poems about the natural world

Do you have a favourite poem? Perhaps you can recall a poem that you particularly enjoyed reading, or with which you felt a special connection. Think of how the poet used words to express his or her ideas. What made this piece of writing a "poem"? What makes poetry different from other types of literature?

Many types of writing follow precise rules, and these types of writing are often easy to describe. When someone uses the words "sentence", "paragraph", "essay", "novel", or "autobiography", we have a fairly clear idea in our minds about what those types of writing are. But a poem is much harder to define.

Take a moment to skim through and compare the poems in this book. They span a wide variety of forms and styles. A poem may only be a few lines long, or it may take up more than a page. It may be organized in blocks of text, or **stanzas**, or it may not be divided in any way.

Some poems follow a precise pattern of rhyming words, or a specific **rhythm** with a certain number of beats per line. Other poems do not follow any pattern at all, and some sound like natural, spoken language. One of the best things about poetry is its freedom of form. Poets can choose from many types of poetry and many different devices to achieve the effect they want in their writing.

POINTS OF VIEW

It is important to remember that there is no "right way" to interpret a poem. When you read a poem for the first time, you may discover something that other readers have not seen. Each reader may see the poem from a different point of view, depending on his or her age, culture, or life experiences. Everyone's understanding of a poem is unique.

The poet's purpose

A poem may affect different readers in different ways, but poets usually want to achieve something specific through their writing. They have a particular **theme** or idea that they want the reader to understand. To express these ideas, poets can use a range of different features in their writing. Such features include the **context**, language, and **structure** of the poem. They can all help the poet get across his or her message.

The context

As you read a poem, think about its context (the time and setting in which it takes place). Context can affect meaning – the ideas the poet wants to share with the reader. The context is especially important in poems about the natural world. In a nature poem, the reader may experience the sights, sounds, and smells of a natural environment – a dark forest, a rolling meadow, a raging river, or a placid lake.

THE PASSING OF TIME

The time in which a poem is set may also be significant. Is it set in the early light of dawn, the bright midday sunshine, or the depths of night? Does the poem suggest the warmth of summer or the hard chill of winter? The time setting might even change over the course of the poem. This is especially true if the poet wants to describe the effects of the passage of time or the changes in an environment over a long period.

Poems about the natural world

Many writers look to the natural world for inspiration. So, how is a "nature poet" different from other people who write about nature? Scientists such as biologists, ecologists, and chemists are also observers of nature. They collect data about the natural world, and use this to answer questions and solve problems. They then write about their findings in books, reports, and journals. Poets take a different approach. They look for a deeper understanding of the natural world. They link it with human emotions, desires, successes, or losses.

Nature can teach us something about ourselves, but it can also reflect the wider human experience. Poems can help us find this connection. A dramatic storm could resemble the turmoil within a troubled soul. A fierce animal might express the wilder or more violent qualities of humans. A flock of graceful birds may reflect the mind of a person who is trying to find peace in the world.

Poetry can also reveal the value of nature to human life. Science can demonstrate the impact of human activities on the environment, but poetry can express the deeper reasons for protecting nature. A poet may describe the grandeur of a mighty redwood tree or the detail of a tiny insect. Such descriptions remind us how important it is to protect these wonderful things.

Poetry can reveal nature in all its impressive detail. "I am in awe of your self-possessed beauty" writes Nikki Giovanni in her poem about an insect (see page 44).

Analysing poetry: Point, Evidence, Explain (P.E.E.)

There may be occasions when you are asked to analyse poetry – to read it carefully and explain what you think are the poet's intentions. At the end of your analysis, you will need to draw conclusions about what the poet was trying to do.

Writing about poetry is more effective when you use a method known as "Point, Evidence, Explain" (P.E.E.). Each statement, or point, that you make should be supported by evidence. This evidence is usually the actual words from the poem. You must then explain how the evidence supports the point you are making.

P.E.E. AND PERSONIFICATION

If you were writing about Emily Dickinson's poem "A Bird came down the Walk" (see page 21), you might make the point that the poem expresses a personal connection with nature. To make this connection, the poem uses **personification** – a literary device in which animals are given human characteristics. As evidence, you would quote words from the poem: a bird "let a beetle pass". You would then explain that deliberately allowing a beetle to pass is something that a human would do, not an animal. By using personification, Dickinson is expressing a close connection between people and nature.

As you read the descriptions of the poems in this book, think about these questions:

- What are the important points made about each poem?
- What evidence is used to support each point?
- What is the effect of this evidence on the reader, or how does it support the point being made?
- What else can you say or add to this point? Does it link to other ideas within the poem?

"The Tyger"

"**The Tyger**" is one of the best-known poems in the English language. It is a powerful piece of writing – not only in its striking description of this terrifying beast, but also in the questions it asks about God and nature.

A creature from a distant land

When William Blake wrote this poem in the late 18th century, he had probably never seen a tiger in the wild. A tiger's natural habitat is the forests of India and Southeast Asia, many thousands of miles from England, where Blake lived. There might have been a few tigers in circuses and zoos, but even this would have been rare in Blake's time. The vivid image of this beast that emerges in the poem, therefore, was a product of the poet's imagination. He may have used the alternative spelling, "tyger", to express the animal's exotic or foreign nature.

"The Tyger" was first published in 1794, in Blake's collection of poems called *Songs of Experience*. He illustrated the verses himself.

Symbolism in the poem

To Blake, the tiger is not simply a wild animal, but a symbol of some greater part of the natural world. It may even be the essence of nature itself. As you read the poem, think about this **symbolism** and the picture of the tiger that Blake wants you to imagine. His words conjure images of a bright, blazing, consuming fire. What do you think the tiger's fiery appearance represents? What ideas come to mind as you read?

We often associate fire with destruction, disorder, and chaos. However, Blake wants the reader to see something positive as well. For him, fire is a symbol of creative energy. With its blazing appearance, the tiger represents a force that is not only wild and uncontrolled, but also very creative. Blake wants us to be in awe of the animal's beauty, strength, and power.

"The Tyger"

by William Blake

Tyger! Tyger! burning bright
In the forests of the night,
What immortal hand or eye
Could frame thy fearful symmetry?

In what distant deeps or skies
Burnt the fire of thine eyes?
On what wings dare he aspire?
What the hand dare sieze the fire?

And what shoulder, & what art.
Could twist the sinews of thy heart?
And when thy heart began to beat,
What dread hand? & what dread feet?

What the hammer? what the chain?
In what furnace was thy brain?
What the anvil? what dread grasp
Dare its deadly terrors clasp?

When the stars threw down their spears,
And watered heaven with their tears,
Did he smile his work to see?
Did he who made the Lamb make thee?

Tyger! Tyger! burning bright
In the forests of the night,
What immortal hand or eye
Dare frame thy fearful symmetry?

WORDS YOU MAY NOT KNOW

Tyger: this was an old-fashioned way of spelling "tiger" even in
Blake's time. Many scholars have wondered why the poet chose
this spelling. What do you think?

symmetry: an object has symmetry if it has equal sides that mirror each
other. It can also mean that an object is well-balanced.

Rhetoric in the poem

Did you notice that the poem is structured as a series of questions? These are **rhetorical questions**, intended to provoke debate and discussion rather than requiring an answer. It is as though Blake is having a conversation with the tiger. Really, however, he expects his readers to think about the questions themselves.

Consider the question "What immortal hand or eye / Could frame thy fearful symmetry?" Blake is asking us to imagine a being (God) that has the power to create a beautiful but terrifying beast like a tiger. The questions continue right to the end of the poem, when Blake asks "Did he who made the Lamb make thee?" Again, we are expected to think about what type of creator could make a world that includes a creature as gentle as a lamb and one as fearsome as a tiger.

P.E.E.: DUAL NATURES

Point: "The Tyger" describes God as having a dual nature – both gentle and violent.

Evidence: the tiger, made by God, is described as being "fearful" and capable of "deadly terrors". However, Blake also asks "Did he who made the Lamb make thee?"

Explain: Blake shows us that God made both the tiger – a ferocious, destructive animal – and the gentle lamb. The poet is saying that God is capable of creating things that are both peaceful and violent.

Blake's unique philosophy

It is difficult to clearly summarize Blakes's philosophy and beliefs. Many people consider him to be a product of the **Enlightenment**. During this period, people began to base their ideas on science and reason rather than old traditions. Blake's own life and thought were full of contradictions. He frequently spoke out against organized religion, even though he considered the Bible important. Indeed, Blake used this holy book as a source of inspiration for his work. He also questioned the faith that many Enlightenment thinkers placed in scientific laws. To Blake, creativity and freedom were more important than science and reason.

USING RHYTHM TO EXPRESS IDEAS

"The Tyger" uses very simple rhyme and **metre** (the pattern of **stressed** and unstressed syllables in a line). This creates a strong feeling of rhythm. Most of the lines in the poem have exactly seven syllables, which alternate between stressed and unstressed:

— ‿ — ‿ — ‿ —

Tyger! Tyger! burning bright

However, six of the lines (4, 10, 11, 18, 20, and 24) have eight syllables, the first of which is unstressed. This change from the typical rhythm scheme adds emphasis to the ideas expressed in these lines.

Notice also how the simple rhythm of the poem has an effect almost like the beating of a blacksmith's hammer as the image of the tiger takes shape. It is as if Blake wants the reader to see the tiger as an object forged in the heat of a **foundry**!

Blake lived during a period of great industry in Britain, when major developments were made in areas such as manufacturing and metalworking.

Forging a tiger

Blake lived and worked at the start of the **Industrial Revolution**. New inventions such as steam engines were rapidly changing the way people lived. Blake evokes the power of industry in the fourth stanza. Here, the process of creating the tiger is compared to the forging of iron. It is as if the tiger's brain is a lump of glowing hot iron emerging from a furnace. Can you picture his steel claws being pounded out by a blacksmith on a huge **anvil**?

The poet is clearly struck by fear and awe of this terrifying beast. But the poem is also a celebration of the process of creation. Blake describes the tiger as an amazing device, created by a brilliant inventor, who devised its twisted sinews, blazing eyes, and grasping claws.

Think about this
Protecting tigers

In Blake's time, tigers were viewed as fearsome creatures. Today, these beautiful animals are endangered and need our protection. At the start of the 20th century, approximately 100,000 tigers lived in the wild. Today there are fewer than 4,000 worldwide because of hunting and habitat destruction. Why do you think it is important to protect tigers? What can be done to help them?

WILLIAM BLAKE

1757–1827

Born: London, England

During his lifetime, **William Blake** was better known as an illustrator of books than as a writer. He developed many of his own techniques for creating illustrations for his books. He considered these images to be almost as important as the poems themselves. Blake did not print the words to his poems using type, but painted them on the page almost as if they were part of the images. His work as a printer and engraver of books allowed him to meet many other writers and philosophers. This helped him develop his own unique beliefs.

Blake believed that religious faith was a personal matter. In his writing, he attempted to express a direct connection between God and humans, or between body and soul.

Did you know? Blake was considered something of an oddball – even a madman – during his own time. Today, however, he is regarded as one of the most creative and original artists and writers that ever lived.

"High Waving Heather"

"High Waving Heather" describes a powerful, **tumultuous** storm, with high winds, thunder, lightning, and overflowing rivers. However, the poem is more than just a description of a storm and its effects. The wild weather is a **metaphor** for the human soul. The features of a storm are compared to the features of the restless spirit.

USING VERBS TO CREATE IMAGERY

When writing a poem, sometimes a poet will deliberately choose certain types of words. For example, a poet may decide to use vivid adjectives such as "bright", "withered", or "majestic" to paint a picture in the reader's mind (**imagery**). In this poem, however, Brontë does not use many adjectives. Instead, she uses a lot of verbs to describe the tumult of nature: "roaring", "flying", "sighing", "defying", "rending", "descending". The poem has been described as a "frenzy of movement" or a "torrent of verbs". These verbs create a feeling of constant, restless movement.

"High Waving Heather"

by Emily Brontë

High waving heather, 'neath stormy blasts bending,
Midnight and moonlight and bright shining stars;
Darkness and glory rejoicingly blending,
Earth rising to heaven and heaven descending,
Man's spirit away from its drear dongeon sending,
Bursting the fetters and breaking the bars.

All down the mountain sides, wild forest lending
One mighty voice to the life-giving wind;
Rivers their banks in the jubilee rending,
Fast through the valleys a reckless course wending,
Wider and deeper their waters extending,
Leaving a desolate desert behind.

Shining and lowering and swelling and dying,
Changing for ever from midnight to noon;
Roaring like thunder, like soft music sighing,
Shadows on shadows advancing and flying,
Lightning-bright flashes the deep gloom defying,
Coming as swiftly and fading as soon.

WORDS YOU MAY NOT KNOW

heather: this purple flowering plant flourishes in the area of Yorkshire
where Emily Brontë grew up. As the wind blew across the heather,
it may have looked like rolling waves on the sea.

dongeon: this is an **archaic** (outdated) spelling of "dungeon". In the
Middle Ages, a dungeon was the underground cellar beneath a
castle, often used as a prison. The dungeon was probably the most
secure part of the castle.

jubilee: this is a grand celebration of an important anniversary, such
as the 50th anniversary of a monarch's coronation.

Escaping from tragedy

Emily Brontë's mother died in 1821, when Emily was very young. Her two oldest sisters died shortly after their mother. The four surviving children of the Brontë family escaped the sadness of their home by writing about magical, fantasy-filled worlds. They created elaborate stories and adventures, and acted them out. Their early tales were about a fictional place called Angria. Later, they wrote about an imaginary island called Gondal. Emily continued writing about this fantasy land even after she grew up.

Perhaps "High Waving Heather", like the Gondal stories, was inspired by tragedy and loss. The wildness of nature expressed in the poem may symbolize a troubled soul struggling to escape from an unhappy life. Brontë also uses the image of a castle dungeon to symbolize the body in which the human spirit may be trapped.

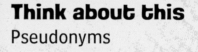

Think about this
Pseudonyms

Emily Brontë did not publish her writing under her own name. She used the **pseudonym** Ellis Bell. Most people at the time thought that women were not intelligent enough to write and publish any type of literature that was worth reading. Interestingly, the first volume in which this poem appeared received good reviews, but only sold two copies! Why do you think this was?

COUNTERPOINT AND CONTRASTS

Counterpoint is the technique of describing two very different objects or attributes, often within the same line. In "High Waving Heather", Brontë uses counterpoint to increase the sense of conflict and turmoil. For example, the wind has a "mighty voice" and the river is "roaring like thunder". However, the river is also "like soft music sighing". These contrasts in sounds may represent the difference between the noisy confusion of nature and the quiet of the soul.

Constant change and motion

"High Waving Heather" is a poem of constant and relentless movement. Each stanza descibes a different state in a seemingly endless cycle of motion. The poem refuses to let the reader escape from this unbroken cycle.

In this poem, nature is constantly in motion, driven by a "life-giving wind". The light reflecting off the rushing water is compared to a joyful celebration. The poet seems to be saying that through this wind, nature allows the spirit to leave the body. The storm invites the spirit to abandon its earthly body and roll through the landscape on a moonlit journey. What do you think Brontë means when she refers to the wind as "life-giving"? Is it life-giving because it is created by God, or because it moves all things? We are left to ponder this question.

EMILY BRONTË

1818–1848

Born: Thornton, England

Emily Brontë was the fifth of six children in her family. Her father worked for the Church of England in the village of Haworth in Yorkshire, where the family moved in 1824. Emily's early years were marked by tragedy. Her mother died in 1821, and her two oldest sisters, Maria and Elizabeth, also died young. After this, the four younger children (Charlotte, Emily, Anne, and Patrick) were educated at home by their father and their aunt.

When she was 20 years old, Emily moved to the Yorkshire town of Halifax to become a teacher. However, she did not stay away for long. She soon returned home, where she occupied herself with housework, teaching Sunday school, and studying. While at home, Emily enjoyed writing plays and stories with her sisters. At the same time, though, she wrote poetry which she kept to herself in private notebooks.

Her sister Charlotte found these notebooks in 1845 and insisted that Emily should try to publish her poetry. The following year, the three Brontë sisters published a collected volume of their poetry under the pseudonyms Currer, Ellis, and Acton Bell. They thought they would get more respect for their work if people believed they were men.

Emily was only 18 years old when she wrote the poem "High Waving Heather".

In 1847, Emily published her first and only novel, *Wuthering Heights* – a dramatic story about the destructive power of love. At the time, the novel received mixed literary reviews, but it is now considered a masterpiece of British literature. Sadly, Emily died of tuberculosis in 1848, and did not live to see her genius as a writer recognized.

Did you know? The Brontë sisters attempted to start a school in their home, but it was unsuccessful because the area they lived in was too remote.

Think about this
A family of great authors

Emily's sister Charlotte was also a great novelist. She is best known for *Jane Eyre*, one of the best-loved novels from the period. Emily was motivated to publish her own novel partly because of the success of *Jane Eyre*. *Wuthering Heights* went to print shortly after Charlotte's book. Have you ever been inspired by a friend or family member to write or create something?

This is a page from one of Emily Brontë's poetry notebooks, containing poems about the fantasy island of Gondal.

"A Bird came down the Walk"

Sometimes the beauty of a poem lies in the simplicity of its subject. This poem describes a moment when the poet comes across a bird on the pavement near her home. Emily Dickinson believed that pausing to take notice of a bird – or an earthworm, or a beetle – was just as important as observing the grand, the powerful, or the majestic in nature.

The world outside her door

Dickinson is known for her keen observations of the natural world, but her poetry does not focus on the grandeur of nature. She does not describe deep forests, wide canyons, or high mountains. Nor does she depict dramatic events such as hurricanes or earthquakes. Her poems are subtle reflections on small encounters with nature right outside the door of her home. They may be with a bird, a flower, or an insect that she noticed on an ordinary day. The world that Dickinson describes is often referred to as a **microcosm** – a small world that reflects the wider world.

As you read this poem, think about the event it describes. Dickinson is simply witnessing a bird landing on the ground in front of her. It eats a worm, looks around, then flies away. The poet was not outside at that moment deliberately seeking inspiration from nature for her poetry. She just happened to be taking a walk when the bird crossed her path and gobbled up a worm. This brief moment was enough for Dickinson to build a great poem around.

PERSONIFICATION

In describing this bird, Dickinson uses the literary device of personification. The bird appears to politely step aside to let a beetle pass, as a human might do. This apparently human-like behaviour is contrasted with its initial act of biting a worm in half and gobbling it up. The contradiction in behaviour reminds us that this is a wild creature with a raw, natural spirit.

"A Bird came down the Walk"

by Emily Dickinson

A Bird came down the Walk—
He did not know I saw—
He bit an Angleworm in halves
And ate the fellow, raw,

And then he drank a Dew
From a convenient Grass—
And then hopped sidewise to the Wall
To let a Beetle pass—

He glanced with rapid eyes
That hurried all around—
They looked like frightened Beads, I thought—
He stirred his Velvet Head

Like one in danger, Cautious,
I offered him a Crumb
And he unrolled his feathers
And rowed him softer home—

Than Oars divide the Ocean,
Too silver for a seam—
Or Butterflies, off Banks of Noon
Leap, plashless as they swim.

WORDS YOU MAY NOT KNOW

Angleworm: an angleworm is simply another name for an earthworm.
In Dickinson's time, they were often referred to as angleworms
because they were used as bait for fishing ("angler" is another
word for a fisherman).

plashless: like many poets, Dickinson was fond of creating new words
when no existing word expressed exactly what she wanted. Such
words are called **neologisms**. Here, Dickinson wanted to express
the silent "swimming" of the butterflies in the air. The word
"plashless" suggests a kind of swimming without making a splash.

An instant of time

How many seconds pass as Dickinson watches this bird? Probably less than a minute. Perhaps even less than 10 seconds. But those few seconds reveal a lot to Dickinson about the bird. It hunts for food (eating the angleworm raw). It gets water from the dew on a piece of grass. It interacts with other creatures (stepping aside to let a beetle pass). Its eyes dart about cautiously, looking for signs of danger. What seems to fascinate Dickinson most is the bird's flight – she compares its wings to oars rowing a boat on an ocean.

These few moments do not reveal any deep insight about the natural world. There is no important message or lesson to be learned. The poem simply describes an encounter in which Dickinson sees a glimpse of nature in its true, wild state.

RHYTHM AND RHYME

Dickinson wrote many of her poems in a basic **iambic trimeter** pattern. This means that each line consists of three rhythmic units, with two syllables in each unit:

1	*2*	*3*	
A Bird	*came down*	*the Walk—*	

1	*2*	*3*	
He did	*not know*	*I saw—*	

This basic rhythm scheme is occasionally interrupted by four-unit lines:

1	*2*	*3*	*4*
He bit	*an An*	*gle worm*	*in halves*

The rhyme scheme is ABCB: the second and fourth lines in the stanza rhyme (B), but the first and third do not (A and C). Such a simple structure emphasizes the simplicity of the moment:

> *And then he drank a Dew*
> *From a convenient Grass—*
> *And then hopped sidewise to the Wall*
> *To let a Beetle pass—*

Writing for herself

When Dickinson first started writing poetry, she had no intention of publishing it or even showing it to others. She wrote just for her own pleasure. In fact, most of her poetry was not discovered until after her death. She rarely wrote about her own beliefs or influences, whether in her poetry or in her letters to friends.

Some scholars believe that Dickinson was a **transcendentalist** – someone who trusts in the purity and goodness of people and the natural world. A transcendentalist believes that social institutions such as religions and political parties are not always good for society. Other scholars have claimed that Dickinson did not follow any particular philosophy or tradition. They think her poetry was not intended to persuade others of any particular point of view.

The poem describes a few interactions with a single bird on a pavement. But when the bird takes off, Dickinson sees wildness in its eating habits and the beauty of its flight.

"GERMAN" CAPITALIZATION

Dickinson studied German as a young woman. This may be why she capitalized certain nouns in her poems, even ones that are not names. In German, non-proper nouns are sometimes capitalized. She may have used this technique to emphasize the importance of certain ordinary objects (such as the angleworm in the poem), or to emphasize the physical size of an object.

*He bit an **A**ngleworm in halves*

In the first editions of Dickinson's poetry, the capitalization was changed to meet the standard rules of English at the time. But in modern publications, Dickinson's poems are written true to her original manuscripts.

Leabharlanna Poiblí Chathair Baile Átha Cliath

EMILY DICKINSON

1830–1886

Born: Amherst, Massachusetts, USA

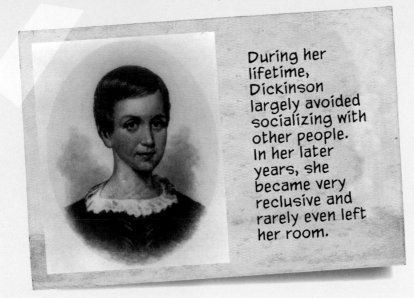

During her lifetime, Dickinson largely avoided socializing with other people. In her later years, she became very reclusive and rarely even left her room.

Emily Dickinson never aspired to become one of the world's greatest poets – she did not even intend her poetry to be published. She demonstrated through her life and work that it is not necessary to live an eventful or well-travelled life to write great poetry.

Dickinson's mother, Emily Norcross Dickinson, was a frail woman with no strong emotional ties to her children. Dickinson was closer to her father, Edward, who was a prominent lawyer. However, his job often took him away from home and Dickinson's childhood was probably very lonely.

Dickinson's father believed that even though a woman's place was in the home, girls should still be educated so that they would be suitable wives. At his direction, she studied at Amherst Academy and later at Mount Holyoke Female Seminary. Afterwards, she returned to the family home in Amherst, where she spent the rest of her life.

By the time Dickinson was in her thirties, she had become very **reclusive**. She shied away from appearing in public or even speaking to guests in her own house. Some people have suggested that she had an illness that stopped her associating with other people. But others believe that Dickinson simply lived alone so she could dedicate herself to her poetry. Her writing reveals a deeply **introspective** soul, someone who was very perceptive about the world around her.

Dickinson kept up with her friends and family through letter-writing. She communicated with one of her closest friends, Susan Gilbert, almost entirely by letters, even though they were next-door neighbours! Gilbert was one of the few people who had the chance to read and review Dickinson's poems. In 1890, she helped publish the first collection of these poems, after Dickinson's death from a kidney disease.

It is not surprising that Dickinson wrote about nature. She studied science from a young age. She created a book with pressed flowers representing over 400 species of plants. She would often send small bunches of flowers to her friends and family to accompany the letters that she wrote.

Did you know? Before she died, Emily instructed her sister Lavinia to destroy her papers after her death. While searching Emily's room, Lavinia uncovered more than 1,700 poems in a chest! Fortunately, Lavinia ignored her sister's instructions, and we are able to enjoy this wealth of great poetry.

Emily Dickinson's house in Amherst is now a museum dedicated to her life and work.

"The Wild Swans at Coole"

The focus of this poem is a particular group of swans that fascinated W. B. Yeats as he visited their nesting site each year. The poem tries to paint an image in the reader's mind of how these majestic birds appeared to the poet. But the poem is as much about the poet himself as it is about the graceful swans.

Nature as a "constant"

Many nature poems focus on the changes that occur in the natural world. Instead, in this poem Yeats highlights the lack of change in nature, year after year. The swans are a "constant" and it is the poet himself who changes, not nature. Because the swans behave the same way each time Yeats sees them, they offer a way for him to measure the changes in his own life.

Throughout the course of this poem, Yeats reflects on the great changes that have occurred in his life. He has aged since he first saw the swans. He has endured the ups and downs of relationships and personal history. Meanwhile, the swans have stayed much the same as they always were. Their beauty and their companionship remain strong. The swans will stay as they are for many years beyond this moment. In a sense they are **immortal** while the poet's life is **mutable** – constantly changing and eventually fading.

ALLITERATION

Carefully read the fourth stanza of the poem, and listen for any patterns in the words chosen by the poet. The poem uses **alliteration**, or the repetition of word sounds and letters within a line. Alliteration can give a poem a musical quality, or it can connect certain words that express a particular image or thought. For example, Yeats's line "wander where they will" repeats the "w" sound, which seems to echo the fluidity of the swans' movements.

What other examples of alliteration can you find in this poem? How do they enhance the poem's meaning?

"The Wild Swans at Coole"

by William Butler Yeats

The trees are in their autumn beauty,
The woodland paths are dry,
Under the October twilight the water
Mirrors a still sky;
Upon the brimming water among the stones
Are nine-and-fifty swans.

The nineteenth autumn has come upon me
Since I first made my count;
I saw, before I had well finished,
All suddenly mount
And scatter wheeling in great broken rings
Upon their clamorous wings.

I have looked upon those brilliant creatures,
And now my heart is sore.
All's changed since I, hearing at twilight,
The first time on this shore,
The bell-beat of their wings above my head,
Trod with a lighter tread.

Unwearied still, lover by lover,
They paddle in the cold
Companionable streams or climb the air;
Their hearts have not grown old;
Passion or conquest, wander where they will,
Attend upon them still.

But now they drift on the still water,
Mysterious, beautiful;
Among what rushes will they build,
By what lake's edge or pool
Delight men's eyes when I awake some day
To find they have flown away?

WORDS YOU MAY NOT KNOW

clamorous: if something is clamorous, it is loud, noisy, and confused.
rushes: these are tall plants with long, slender stems. They often
grow along the shores of wetland areas, and provide shelter for
nesting waterfowl such as swans and geese.

The poet's reflections

In the first stanza of the poem, Yeats establishes its setting. What images do these lines create in your mind? Do they remind you of a crisp, autumn day? What tone does this stanza set for the rest of the poem?

The location of the poem is the estate at Coole in Ireland, home to Lady Augusta Gregory – a well-known Irish writer and a friend of Yeats. It is a cool October day. For 19 years, Yeats has spent his summers at Coole, and now this particular summer has passed. After many years of visiting this tranquil spot to observe the swans, Yeats reflects on the changes that have occurred in both his own life and the world beyond.

At the time this poem was written, World War I was raging. The conflict was tearing Europe apart and destroying millions of lives. Nearly every family in Britain was deeply affected by the war.

Think about this
Swan migration

During their yearly migration, swans travel vast distances – sometimes flying thousands of kilometres without stopping. Their journey usually follows a very precise path, and groups of swans will return to the same places year after year along that path. For this reason, **conservationists** are able to predict exactly where swans can be seen at certain times each year. Just as Yeats notes in his poem, swans truly are an example of regularity in nature. What other examples of regularity or repeating patterns have you observed in nature?

In this poem, Yeats might be reflecting on the war's impact on his own life. Lady Gregory was mourning the death of her only child in the war, and this may have made Yeats consider the temporary nature of human existence.

A meditative setting

The setting of the poem has been described as **meditative**. This means that it provides a tranquil setting for Yeats to reflect on his own existence. Notice how the poet writes that there are exactly 59 swans – he counted them as he watched. Many people use counting as a way of relaxing and meditating. We can imagine Yeats doing the same as he mulls over the changes in his life.

When the swans take off, Yeats describes them as "clamorous". After initially establishing such a tranquil scene, why would he choose this word to describe the swans' flight? In the poem, Yeats is quiet and alone; in contrast, nature is loud and lively. Perhaps Yeats wishes he could join them, but feels trapped in his human existence. The clamorous swans might also represent his own state of mind – the noisy commotion of the birds reflecting his own troubled emotions.

P.E.E.: CREATING A MEDITATIVE SETTING

Point: Yeats is describing a meditative setting in which he can consider his own thoughts.

Evidence: Yeats knows the exact number of the birds, which means he counted them.

Explain: his act of counting is itself meditative – it relaxes the mind and prepares it for deep thought.

World War I (1914–1918) devastated people and landscapes across Europe. The war inspired an outpouring of literature, particularly poetry.

Time and the ageing process

Notice that the poem is set in autumn. This may be a metaphor for the late stage in Yeats's life. The ageing process and the cycle of life are important themes in the poem. In October, the trees are filled with bright colours, yet winter is approaching. We feel the chill in the air and see the lake reflecting the autumn sky. The water is cold, although the swans do not seem to notice. While the setting suggests the ending of life, the swans represent its renewal.

Almost two decades have passed since Yeats first observed the swans on the lake, and although their lives have changed little, his own life has changed a great deal. When he first saw the swans, he walked with lighter steps. When Yeats writes that the swans' hearts are still young, he is actually saying that he feels his own heart has grown older. The swans travel in couples, but Yeats is alone.

As they fly away, the swans – representing beauty, life, and perhaps lost love – are travelling to new destinations. There, they will be admired by other people. Perhaps the swans represent a type of immortality against which the poet is somehow losing a battle. Their beauty will continue after Yeats is no longer there to see it. Building their nests in the rushes, the swans will reproduce and thus remain on Earth.

WILLIAM BUTLER YEATS

1865–1939
Born: Dublin, Ireland

William Butler Yeats was the son of a successful painter in Dublin, Ireland. Yeats himself trained to be a painter. Even after discovering his love of writing poetry, his training in the visual arts may have enhanced his ability to create vivid images in the minds of his readers.

When Yeats was a young man, Ireland was part of the United Kingdom. But Irish nationalism was rising, and many Irish people wanted independence for their country. Yeats was vocally pro-Irish. He used his writing to protest against British rule. He remained active in politics throughout his life, and served as a senator in the Irish Senate for two terms beginning in 1922. During his involvement with the Irish nationalist movement, Yeats fell in love with Maud Gonne, an Irish revolutionary. He proposed to her several times, but she married another man in 1903. Perhaps because of a broken heart, Yeats did not marry until he was 51.

W. B. Yeats was the first Irishman to be awarded the Nobel Prize for Literature, in 1932.

Yeats's abilities as a poet became more developed later in life. Scholars agree that his best work was written when he was an older man. He remained very productive as a writer until his death in 1939.

Did you know? In 1924, Yeats chaired a committee choosing designs for the first currency of the Irish Free State.

"The Groundhog"

Many poems about nature describe how plants and animals affect us when they are alive. A small bird, a ferocious tiger, or a flock of magnificent swans can create powerful emotions in us. But can a plant or animal inspire us even after it is dead? In "The Groundhog", Richard Eberhart shows us that seeing a dead animal as it decays can make us consider our own existence.

The meaning of death and decay

Over the course of this **narrative**, Eberhart observes a groundhog in four different stages of **decomposition**:

1 When he first sees the body in the summer, he observes maggots busily consuming its flesh.
2 He returns in the autumn to find the groundhog a "sodden hulk" – a swollen mass of rotting flesh.
3 The following summer all that is left is hair and bleached bones.
4 The final time he visits the spot, all trace of the groundhog has vanished.

Each stage encourages the poet to ask different questions about life and death. He considers his own mortality, reflects on his place in nature, and eventually accepts the finality of death. In an interview, Eberhart once said: "Death poems are as good as life poems because they are also life poems, written in flesh and blood. Poetry embraces the moment as it flies."

WORDS YOU MAY NOT KNOW

mured: the word "mure" means to enclose or imprison something within walls. This is an archaic word that is not used any more. Poets will often use archaic terms because they work well in the poem, because they conjure up thoughts of another time, or simply because they seem to express an idea best.
geometer: a geometer is someone who is an expert in geometry.

"The Groundhog"

by Richard Eberhart

In June, amid the golden fields,
I saw a groundhog lying dead.
Dead lay he; my senses shook,
And mind outshot our naked frailty.

There lowly in the vigorous summer
His form began its senseless change,
And made my senses waver dim
Seeing nature ferocious in him.

Inspecting close maggots' might
And seething cauldron of his being,
Half with loathing, half with a strange love,
I poked him with an angry stick.

The fever arose, became a flame
And Vigour circumscribed the skies,
Immense energy in the sun,
And through my frame a sunless trembling.

My stick had done nor good nor harm.
Then stood I silent in the day
Watching the object, as before;
And kept my reverence for knowledge

Trying for control, to be still,
To quell the passion of the blood;
Until I had bent down on my knees
Praying for joy in the sight of decay.

And so I left; and I returned
In Autumn strict of eye, to see
The sap gone out of the groundhog,
But the bony sodden hulk remained

But the year had lost its meaning,
And in intellectual chains
I lost both love and loathing,
Mured up in the wall of wisdom.

Another summer took the fields again
Massive and burning, full of life,
But when I chanced upon the spot
There was only a little hair left,

And bones bleaching in the sunlight
Beautiful as architecture;
I watched them like a geometer,
And cut a walking stick from a birch.

It has been three years, now.
There is no sign of the groundhog.
I stood there in the whirling summer,
My hand capped a withered heart,

And thought of China and of Greece,
Of Alexander in his tent;
Of Montaigne in his tower,
Of Saint Theresa in her wild lament.

Time and change

Notice how Eberhart connects his observations of nature with the passage of his own life. Yeats makes a similar connection in "The Wild Swans at Coole". Think about these two poems. How are they similar in their message about the passing of time and the ageing process? How are they different?

Although "The Groundhog" describes the decay of an ordinary animal, watching its body decompose sparks in Eberhart a wide range of emotions. When he first sees the dead groundhog, he is shaken by the realization of how frail life can be. When he notices the maggots devouring the body, he is overcome with an awareness of the energy found in nature. Later, his emotions are calmer, as he compares the lifeless body of the groundhog (drained of its "sap") to the meaning that has been drained from his own life.

On his final visit, Eberhart considers the complexity of the groundhog's bones, describing them as "Beautiful as architecture".

P.E.E.: THE IRONY OF LIFE AND DEATH

Point: Eberhart uses **irony** to show that death can actually be a source of life.

Evidence: he is describing a dead animal as it decays, but the maggots are a "cauldron" of life. Later, he sees the bones as a complex structure that he finds inspiring.

Explain: even in death, the groundhog is full of life.

The poet studies them "like a geometer" – with the eye of a scientist. The bones are of a very precise, technical design, like a building or a machine. This fascination with the bones seems to restore the poet's spirit, inspiring him to cut a walking stick from a tree branch.

Life out of death

Eberhart wrote about death in many of his poems. This might seem like an odd choice of theme, but he used it to communicate important messages about life.

Look carefully at how the groundhog is described in the opening stanzas. It may be dead, but it is not lifeless. In the second and third stanzas, Eberhart recognizes that even in death, its body is full of life. He sees "nature ferocious in him" as the maggots consume the animal's body. This is an example of poetic irony. The poet points out two things that seem to contradict each other, but which in fact show a key idea or truth. Here, Eberhart notes that the body of the dead groundhog provides food for other animals. It is actually a "cauldron" (a large cooking pot) of life.

Think about this
Decomposition

Decomposition is the process by which the bodies of dead plants and animals are broken down into separate chemicals. This decay is essential to our **ecosystem**, because it allows the chemicals to be reused or recycled by other plants and animals.

Decomposition is carried out by many different living things. Worms or insect larvae (such as maggots), bacteria, and fungi eat the tissues of dead plants and animals. They use these nutrients to live and grow. The waste products from their digestion are returned to the soil to provide nutrients for the plants that grow there.

What examples of decomposition have you observed in your own environment? Why is decomposition an important part of the ecosystem?

LITERARY ALLUSIONS

Poets often use historical or literary **allusions**. These are references to people, places, or ideas found in history or other works of literature. The poet usually assumes that the reader knows who or what these things are, and will therefore understand the meaning of the poem. Allusions are intended to offer the reader a richer understanding of the poem, often by placing it in a particular context, or linking it to another story.

Near the end of "The Groundhog", Eberhart reflects that he himself has "withered". He makes allusions to people and events that have also "withered" – they have fallen victim to decay and decline. China and Greece once had great and glorious empires that faded and died. Alexander was a brilliant general who built the largest empire the world had ever seen, but he died as a young man. Montaigne, a great Renaissance philosopher, confined himself to a tower after he grew tired and weary of public life.

In the poem, how are the groundhog's bones similar to Blake's tiger as an act of creation? How are they different?

RICHARD EBERHART

1904–2005

Born: Austin, Minnesota, USA

Richard Eberhart is considered a modern poet, but his writing has been compared to that of 18th-century **Romantics** such as William Blake. These poets placed emotion and imagination above science and reason. Many of Eberhart's ideas and themes may have come from tragedies that he experienced during his childhood. A crisis at his father's place of employment resulted in serious financial problems for his family. When Eberhart was 18, his mother died of lung cancer. These unhappy events early in his life may have caused the preoccupation with death that he later showed in his writing. Eberhart once said that the death of his mother was the event that triggered his career as a poet.

Eberhart's romantic outlook and his preoccupation with death probably originated in his early life experience.

As a young man, Eberhart's life was filled with instability. He showed some promise as a writer while he was a student at Cambridge and Harvard during the 1930s. But his early work met with harsh criticism, and he struggled to find recognition for his writing. Eberhart joined the navy during World War II. When he returned from the war, he worked in his wife's family's shoe-polish company for several years. After he left the company in the 1950s, he was finally able to build a satisfying career as a university professor. During this time, he received many awards for his poetry, including the **Pulitzer Prize** and the National Book Award.

Did you know? In the early 1930s, Eberhart was a tutor to the son of the king of Siam (now Thailand).

"Planting a Sequoia"

The subject of this poem is the careful planting of a tiny **sequoia seedling**. This young tree is perhaps only a few centimetres tall, but the seedling has the potential to become one of nature's most awe-inspiring sights. The sequoia is one of the tallest trees in the world.

The life of a giant

The giant sequoia, the magnificent tree that provides the centrepiece for this poem, is found mainly on the slopes of the Sierra Nevada Mountains in California, USA. Giant sequoias are the world's largest trees in terms of their volume. Their trunks average several metres in diameter and they can stretch to great heights. Sequoias are also among the world's oldest organisms. Many live to be thousands of years old. One of the largest sequoias, located in Sequoia National Park in California, is 75 metres (247 feet) tall, has a trunk 8 metres (27 feet) in diameter, and is estimated to be 3,200 years old!

Compared to a sequoia, which may live thousands of years, Gioia describes the lives of humans as "ephemeral". The tree Gioia plants with his brothers will still be standing long after his family has passed away and been forgotten.

"Planting a Sequoia"

by Dana Gioia

All afternoon my brothers and I have worked in the orchard,
Digging this hole, laying you into it, carefully packing the soil.
Rain blackened the horizon, but cold winds kept it over the Pacific,
And the sky above us stayed the dull gray
Of an old year coming to an end.

In Sicily a father plants a tree to celebrate his first son's birth—
An olive or a fig tree—a sign that the earth has one more life to bear.
I would have done the same, proudly laying new stock into my father's orchard,
A green sapling rising among the twisted apple boughs,
A promise of new fruit in other autumns.

But today we kneel in the cold planting you, our native giant,
Defying the practical custom of our fathers,
Wrapping in your roots a lock of hair, a piece of an infant's birth cord,
All that remains above earth of a first-born son,
A few stray atoms brought back to the elements.

We will give you what we can—our labor and our soil,
Water drawn from the earth when the skies fail,
Nights scented with the ocean fog, days softened by the circuit of bees.
We plant you in the corner of the grove, bathed in western light,
A slender shoot against the sunset.

And when our family is no more, all of his unborn brothers dead,
Every niece and nephew scattered, the house torn down,
His mother's beauty ashes in the air,
I want you to stand among strangers, all young and ephemeral to you,
Silently keeping the secret of your birth.

WORDS YOU MAY NOT KNOW

ephemeral: things that are ephemeral are short-lived, or transient.
They may last less than a day or even a single moment.

Rituals of life and death

Do you remember planting something when you were young – perhaps in your back garden or at school? Was it exciting waiting for it to grow? For Gioia, planting the sequoia is a particularly important event. It is his way of **commemorating** the death of his baby son. It is also a way for him to bring new life into the world – a life that might last long after he and his family are gone.

As you read the first stanza, notice how Gioia uses **diction** (word choice) to create a serious mood: "cold", "blackened", "dull", and "gray". The planting of the sequoia is also described much like a funeral ritual, and the ceremony provides a way for the poet to mourn the loss of his child.

In the second stanza, the tone becomes warmer and lighter. Gioia describes the Italian–American custom of planting an olive or fig tree to celebrate the birth of a child. Part of this custom is to wrap the umbilical cord of an infant around the roots of the tree before planting it. This ritual is a happy event – a celebration of a new life. The third stanza compares this ritual with the planting of the sequoia, describing it as one would describe a religious ceremony. This is how the poet honours the Italian tradition in a way that suits the environment of California, where the sequoia grows.

FREE VERSE

"Planting a Sequoia" is written in **free verse**. This means that it does not follow a set pattern of rhyme or rhythm. Rather, it is written in a way that sounds more like natural speech. However, even though the sentences in the poem are written in this open style, the lines and stanzas form a pattern – each stanza has exactly five lines. Gioia has noted that compressing each stanza into a fixed number of lines forces him to make these lines richer and more interesting.

Poetic irony

This poem is a good example of poetic irony. The planting of the tree begins as a way of mourning the death of a loved one. As the poem progresses, the ceremony becomes a way of celebrating and appreciating life. The sequoia could live for thousands of years, and its beauty will be appreciated by many future generations. The planting of a tree marks the end of one life but the beginning of another. Death is a necessary part of life – one cannot exist without the other.

The oldest known sequoia is estimated to be at least 3,500 years old.

ANCIENT SURVIVORS

Sequoias have incredibly long life spans. Their age is due not only to their large size, but also to chemicals within the wood that protect them from changing conditions. Their thick bark is fire-resistant. It can even shield the trees from a fire that consumes everything else in the forest! In fact, forest fires can help sequoias. They burn away competing tree species and open the sequoia's seed cones to allow new seeds to grow.

Poetry as an expression of life experience

Gioia believes that a poet "necessarily creates out of his or her own life experience", but he has also said that poetry should connect to the reader's life experience as well as the poet's. "Planting a Sequoia" is about a deeply personal experience in Gioia's life. However, he describes it in such a way that the reader can also relate to it closely.

Earth as a giver of life

Gioia writes that the planting of a tree is "a sign that the earth has one more life to bear". This is another example of personification – in this case, giving human qualities to the earth. Gioia is saying that when we plant a tree, not only are we doing something for the earth, but the earth is doing something for us. It is giving new life.

The poem also suggests that there are limits to how much life the earth can give, especially if we don't take care of it. Although "Planting a Sequoia" does not try to teach a lesson about protecting the environment, it does express our connection to our planet, hinting at how much we depend on it.

P.E.E.: CONNECTING LIFE AND DEATH

Point: the planting of the sequoia seedling shows that death is a necessary part of life.

Evidence: Gioia describes the planting much like a burial.

Explain: however, the planting of the seedling marks the end of one life and the beginning of another.

DANA GIOIA

1950–

Born: Los Angeles, California, USA

Gioia once stated in an interview that he believed a poem should be "about us, not about me".

Dana Gioia was the first member of his family to go to university. After earning a BA and an MBA from Stanford University, he built a successful career in business. Gioia was an executive for the General Foods Corporation for many years, before he decided to become a full-time writer and poet. Working in the corporate world might seem unusual for a poet, but Gioia believes this experience has strengthened his writing. He says that when writers and poets have worked at normal jobs, it has "toughened the resolve" and made them stronger individuals.

In addition to his poetry, Gioia has written books and articles about the importance of poetry in American culture. He argues that poetry is not something that can only be appreciated by scholars at universities. He thinks it can be enjoyed by everyone. Through his work, he tries to bring poetry to a wider audience. He writes in a style that appeals to people from many backgrounds.

Did you know? In 2005, Gioia helped set up an event called the Big Read – an initiative to get more Americans reading serious literature.

"The Yellow Jacket"

In some places, "yellow jacket" is the common name for a stinging insect with yellow and black stripes, similar to a bee. Elsewhere, they are known as wasps. In this poem, Nikki Giovanni describes her encounter with one of these insects and the lesson she learns from it.

WORDS YOU MAY NOT KNOW

enforceable: in law, some contracts or agreements between two people are unenforceable – meaning that you cannot force the other person to meet their promises under the contract.

"The Yellow Jacket"

by Nikki Giovanni

We pause in our day
Before completion of evening
Chores
I to cook dinner
And you … I'm not sure
What you do

I empty the birdbaths
Always worrying
A virus or germ
Or unpleasant bacteria may lurk
To do fatal harm
To those who only bring
Their voices in joy
And thanksgiving for fresh water

And you buzz and … quite frankly … annoy
Me as I go about this duty
Fulfilling a contract that was
Never signed and is not at all
Enforceable
But nonetheless a cheerful
Duty to our feathered friends

Recognizing each tree gone
Each bush removed for a deck
Or a patio has left a place
Less welcoming I hope
The birds accept this clean water
As a suitable replacement

I swat at you worried
You will sting
Causing my throat to swell
Blocking my air or
Some other unknown danger
Humans attribute when we hear
Buzzes

You wait … buzz by …
And wait again
Until the water is filled
Where you can sit
Majestically on the edge
And drink

We are not friends
The yellow jacket and I
You will not be tamed
Or trained
Your sound will offer no comfort
Nor your numbers any sense
Of safety

Yet in this evening
Watching you drink
I am in awe
Of your self-possessed
Beauty

Wildlife in a suburban environment

This poem focuses on a very ordinary event in the poet's daily life – an encounter with a wasp in her garden. She sees it while carrying out the simple task of filling a birdbath. It causes her to reflect on her feelings about this irritating insect, as well as the environment around her home.

When Giovanni goes out to fill the birdbath, she feels she has made a contract with the birds to give them fresh water. She is afraid that the water will breed disease if it is not changed. The poet also expresses guilt over the trees and bushes that had to be removed when her garden deck and patio were built. She wants to give something back to nature to make up for this.

By the end of the poem, Giovanni realizes that the water she provides is used not only by the birds, but also by the "harmful" wasp. Her actions have a greater impact than she had realized. She also discovers beauty in a creature that she sees as annoying and potentially harmful.

Tension and repose

In the second half of the poem, Giovanni quickly builds a tense, stressful mood. In the fifth stanza, the thought of being stung by the yellow jacket creates a sense of panic because it could be life-threatening. Do you think she is overreacting to the potential danger?

P.E.E.: CONTRASTING EMOTIONS

Point: the poet realizes she can have two different feelings about the yellow jacket – fear and admiration – and that both can exist at the same time.

Evidence: the structure of the poem takes us from a point when the poet only feels fear and annoyance, thinking she will be stung, to a point where she can calmly contemplate the yellow jacket as it drinks, and is struck by its quiet beauty.

Explain: observing nature can sometimes involve seemingly contradictory emotions, but in fact these emotions can be felt at the same time.

In the remaining stanzas, however, a feeling of calm sets in. As her panic subsides, Giovanni realizes that although she will never be friendly with the yellow jacket, she should not fear it. By the end of the poem, she is able to watch it in the quiet of the evening, and admire its beauty as it drinks from the birdbath.

Think about this
Yellow jacket or honeybee?

Many people confuse yellow jackets with honeybees because they look similar, but bees and wasps are two entirely different orders of insects. Many species of both bees and wasps live in large colonies, where a queen produces offspring. Many species of both can also sting other animals. But yellow jackets are often more aggressive than bees and they can sting more than once. Honeybees are much less likely to sting unless provoked, and they will usually die after a single sting.

Yellow jackets are an important part of the ecosystem, because they are pollinators and control the populations of other insects. What other organisms do you know that appear harmful in some ways, but are actually beneficial to our environment?

Honeybees collect nectar from flowers to make honey that is stored as food. Many yellow jackets feed on other insects, although adult wasps also feed on nectar.

Conflicting emotions

Over the course of the poem, Giovanni shows conflicting feelings about the yellow jacket. In the beginning, she is irritated by it as it interrupts her task. Later, she describes how she is afraid of being stung. At the end of the poem, despite her worry and irritation over this creature, she also acknowledges its "self-possessed beauty".

Giovanni recognizes that in our interactions with nature we can experience a range of emotions – some of them irrational (not logical), and some of them contradictory. Compare the feelings expressed in "The Yellow Jacket" to Blake's feelings towards the tiger in his poem. Can you see a similar conflict of emotions? Is it possible to experience both fear and appreciation for certain things in nature? Do you have conflicting emotions towards any plants or animals?

THE NARRATIVE FORM

Giovanni has said that her favourite type of poetry is the narrative form. A narrative is a story, told in a sequence of events, with a beginning, a middle, and an end (or a problem, climax, and conclusion). It may be difficult to recognize the narrative in "The Yellow Jacket", because it describes such a brief period of time, but in fact it does relay a sequence of events.

Giovanni goes out in the evening before dinner to fill a birdbath. She sees the wasp and tries to swat it away. The wasp defies her and lands on the birdbath to drink. She then calmly contemplates the wasp drinking. During this short time span, the poet makes important realizations about herself and the natural world. Compare Giovanni's narrative to Dickinson's in "A Bird came down the Walk". What similarities can you see?

In the poem, Giovanni describes how she feels a duty to fill the water in the birdbath regularly; she establishes a relationship with the wildlife in her environment.

NIKKI GIOVANNI

1943–

Born: Knoxville, Tennessee, USA

Giovanni was a leading poet of the "Black Renaissance" – a flourishing of art, music, and literature among African Americans during the 1960s.

As a student at Fisk University in the 1960s, **Nikki Giovanni** was very active in the civil rights movement. The poetry she wrote during this time was heavily influenced by the struggle against racism in the United States. Many of these poems touched on such subjects as the assassinations of Martin Luther King, Malcolm X, and Robert Kennedy.

In the 1970s, Giovanni served as a professor of literature at Rutgers University. During this time, she committed much of her career to writing poetry for children. Many of her poems since then have focused on teaching children African American history and dealing with the social issues facing black youth.

Giovanni is particularly fond of rap and hip hop music. She believes that these forms are an important part of African American musical heritage, and they have had a strong influence on her writing. She said: "If culture was a railroad, I can see the tracks running from the Spirituals to the Hip Hop Nation."

Did you know? Giovanni has received numerous awards for her writing, including several NAACP Image Awards, the Langston Hughes Award for Distinguished Contributions to Arts and Letters, and the Rosa Parks Woman of Courage Award.

Putting it all together

The poems in this book are written in a wide variety of styles – some with complex rhythms, others in a more natural language. They also cover a variety of subjects, from tiny insects to ferocious tigers and the massive sequoia tree. But although the content of these poems varies greatly, they share common themes that are universal in nature.

Death and change in life

A frequent theme in nature poetry is the life cycle. In the natural world, all life is temporary and death is a necessary part of life. The most obvious example is in "The Groundhog", where the poet's observations of an animal's slow decomposition inspire him to reflect on his own mortality. They also make him realize that life and death are intertwined. Even in death, the groundhog is a "cauldron" of life.

A similar message is found in "Planting a Sequoia". There, the poet recognizes the interdependence of life and death. In planting a seedling, he is mourning the death of his son. But the act of planting a tree is also the start of a new life – one that will outlive his family and which will inspire future generations.

Beauty in small things

Some nature poems prove that even the smallest things in the natural world can be beautiful and profound. Emily Dickinson wrote about the microcosm of nature just outside her home. She built her poetry around observations of small and seemingly ordinary plants and animals. Dickinson recognized that even their simple activities and interactions can teach us about the relationship between humans and nature.

"The Yellow Jacket" seems to be a continuation of this tradition, describing the poet's encounter with a common insect in her garden. In watching this insect – first swatting at it in irritation, and then calmly watching it drink – Giovanni makes important discoveries about herself and recognizes the hidden beauty in supposedly hazardous organisms.

Good and evil

Nature poetry sometimes addresses the conflict between good and evil, and explores how that conflict is reflected in nature. "The Tyger" describes how a ferocious beast can be both destructive and creative – it has characteristics that are both positive and negative. Blake also contrasts the tiger with the gentle lamb, pointing out that both these animals, one violent and the other peaceful, are the products of the same creator.

To a limited extent, "The Yellow Jacket" also expresses this conflict. At the beginning of the poem, the insect is an enemy, with the potential to sting and even cause death. At the end, the poet refuses to call the yellow jacket a "friend", but she acknowledges its beauty. The yellow jacket has both positive and negative qualities that the poet feels compelled to accept.

The language of nature poetry

We have also seen how certain tools are used across many poems to develop themes and messages about nature.

Imagery. Nature poets often use detailed imagery to create settings, establish moods, or connect readers to their subjects. They use vivid adjectives to draw a picture in the reader's mind. For example, the language of "The Tyger" produces an unforgettable image of the fiery, snarling beast emerging from the forest. Effective imagery can also be created by word choices and other poetic techniques. In "High Waving Heather", verbs are used to describe the swirling storm. In some poems, the sounds of the words – as well as their meanings – are used to create imagery. In "The Wild Swans at Coole", alliteration conveys the sound and motion of the swans in flight.

Personification. An important purpose of many nature poems is to convey the close connection between humans and nature. Personification is sometimes used to show this, by giving human qualities to plants or animals. In "A Bird came down the Walk", the bird is described almost as a neighbour that the poet has met while taking a walk. It eats its lunch, steps aside to let a beetle pass, and watches the poet warily before flying away. In "Planting a Sequoia", personification is used to describe the earth almost as a living being that will give back to us if we preserve it.

Rhythm. In poetry, rhythm can serve many purposes beyond organizing the words and sounds in a pattern. As we can see in "The Tyger", rhythm can give emphasis to certain words by setting them apart from the rest of the poem in the number of beats per line (see page 11). Rhythm can also emphasize the imagery that the poet wishes to create in the reader's mind. In particular, it often helps the reader to really feel the action being described. In "The Tyger", the rhythm mimics the sound of the blacksmith's hammer as it strikes hot metal. In "A Bird came down the Walk", a simple rhythmic structure complements a simple theme.

Allusion. Literary allusions are usually references to people, places, or events in human culture. They can be used to develop a richer context and define a connection between humans and nature. In "The Groundhog", the poet refers to historical figures who receded into history, just as plants and animals eventually die. Including them in the poem reminds us of the temporary nature of human life. In "Planting a Sequoia", allusion is used in a different way – referring to an Italian custom of planting a tree after the birth of a child. By comparing this ritual to the planting of the sequoia (done to mourn the loss of a child), the poet expresses a necessary relationship between life and death.

Write your own nature poem

Poetry is all around us. We hear it every day in the lyrics of songs. Inspiring lines from memorable poems are often quoted in books and speeches. Poems have been written about almost every subject imaginable. They can be written in a rhyming pattern or they can sound like natural language. Poems can be long and complex or only a few lines. Some poems are less than a single sentence on a page!

Poetry does not have to follow precise rules. Nor does it need to be sophisticated or complicated. However, every word in the poem should have a purpose – it should reflect your deliberate intent. The poem should also try to express your true feelings, not someone else's.

The subject matter

As in almost any type of writing, it is usually best to start by writing about something you know well or have experienced personally. Remember that much of Emily Dickinson's poetry was written about the plants and animals she observed around her own home. A poem may also be about a natural environment that you visited, such as a park, a nature trail, or a beach.

A nature poem often strives to build a close connection between the reader and nature. But it does not need to describe everything that one might experience in a particular environment. It could pick only one item – or even just one feature of that item. For example, if you were writing a poem about a visit to the beach, the entire poem could be about a single seashell that you found, or about the motion of the waves as they crashed on the shore. In nature, even small or seemingly insignificant things can teach us about the environment and our connection to it.

Recording ideas – the poet's journal

Nearly every writer experiences "writer's block" at some point – that moment when we get stuck and cannot seem to find inspiration or ideas. Staring at the blank page or computer screen will not help you move forward!

A powerful source of ideas for many writers is a journal – a notebook or program on your mobile phone that you can keep with you to jot down ideas whenever they come to you. You may be walking in the woods one day and see something that fascinates you. A colony of brightly coloured mushrooms on a log might remind you of the diversity of life. Or an insect caught in a spider's web may send a message about life cycles or how different organisms are connected to one another.

A journal is a safe place for you to record your ideas, because no one else will see them and judge them. The journal is for you alone to build a bank of ideas for future writing. Once you have collected a large number of entries in your journal, you can return to those entries for poetry ideas. But remember that an idea that you jotted in your journal is only a touchstone for a poem – a starting point around which to build other ideas.

Build around a central idea

When you begin writing, first try to develop a clear idea of what you want to say to the reader about the subject. What themes or ideas do you want to express? All the other characteristics of the poem should be carefully chosen to support that idea. If you are writing about a terrible loss, you might choose adjectives that create a dark and sombre tone. If you are writing about something in nature that has a particular sound or rhythm, such as a babbling brook or a squawking flock of birds, you may try to use words that convey those attributes. Remember that all the features of a poem – style, form, rhythm, word choice – are crafted by the poet for a purpose: to express his or her deliberate intent.

Use your five senses

The use of imagery is especially important in writing poems about nature. Imagery creates a vivid mental picture of our subject in the mind of the reader. Imagery is not only what we see with our eyes, but what we touch, taste, hear, or smell. We experience nature with every one of our five senses, and effective poetry should use them as well.

Consider the sounds of nature. The natural world is filled with noise, whether it is crashing thunder, the howl of a wolf, or the roar of a waterfall. Poems may not only use adjectives to describe what something sounds like; the words themselves can mimic sounds. The sounds of the words may also generate certain feelings. For example, when Yeats repeats the "w" sound in the line "wander where they will", he wants the reader to feel the gentle, flowing movement of a flock of swans as they float across the sky.

Read more poetry!

One of the best sources of inspiration for poetry is the work of other poets. Poets will often say that at one time or another they were inspired by the writing of some other poet. A poem that you found particularly interesting or exciting could be a source of ideas. For example, you may be struck by the way that Emily Brontë uses verbs to create a tumult of motion in her poem. This may inspire you to use more action words in your own poetry. But remember that other people's writing should only be used as an inspiration. You should try to develop your own unique style and voice as you write.

Bibliography

The following works provided important sources of information for this book:

The Art of Emily Brontë, Anne Smith (Vision Press, 1976)

Blake: A Biography, Peter Ackroyd (Alfred A. Knopf, 1996)

The Book of Yeats's Poems, Hazard Adams (Florida State University Press, 1990)

The Brontës (Literary Lives), Phyllis Bentley (Thames and Hudson, 1969)

The Complete Poems of Emily Brontë, C. W. Hatfield (ed.) (Columbia University Press, 1941)

Critics on Yeats (Readings in Literary Criticism), Raymond Cowell (ed.) (University of Miami Press, 1971)

Discussions of William Blake, John E. Grant (ed.) (D. C. Heath and Company, 1961)

Emily Brontë: Her Life and Her Work, Muriel Spark and Derek Stanford (Coward-McCann, Inc., 1966)

Emily Dickinson, Bradley Steffens (Lucent Books, 1998)

Emily Dickinson and the Image of Home, Jean McClure Mudge (University of Massachusetts Press, 1975)

Emily Dickinson: Singular Poet, Carol Dommermuth-Costa (Lerner Publications Company, 1998)

The Gardens of Emily Dickinson, Judith Farr (Harvard University Press, 2004)

The Poetry of Emily Dickinson, Ruth Miller (Wesleyan University Press, 1968)

A Reader's Guide to William Butler Yeats, John Unterecker, John (Farrar, Strauss & Giroux, 1959)

William Blake (Bloom's Bio Critiques), Harold Bloom (ed.) (Chelsea House Publishers, 2006)

William Blake: The Gates of Paradise, Michael Beardard (Tundra Press, 2006)

Glossary

alliteration repetition of the same sounds at the beginning of words within a sentence, phrase, or line of poetry

allusion reference to a person, place, or event from literature or history

angleworm earthworm

anvil metal block with a flat top used for hammering metals into shape

archaic old-fashioned

clamorous noisy and confused

commemorating doing something special to remember an event or person

conservationist someone who works to protect the natural environment

context setting or surrounding conditions that give meaning to the text

counterpoint contrasting idea that gives meaning to another idea

decomposition breaking down or decaying of dead plant and animal matter

diction choice of words in speech or writing

dongeon underground prison, usually beneath a castle (this is the old-fashioned spelling of the word "dungeon")

ecosystem all the living things in a particular environment

enforceable something that a person can be made to follow or obey

Enlightenment philosophical movement during the 18th century, based on a belief in science and reason

ephemeral lasting only a very short time

foundry place where metal is melted and then shaped into objects

free verse form of poetry that does not have distinct patterns, and is written in the style of natural speech

geometer expert in geometry

heather plant native to England and Scotland, with pink or purple flowers

iambic trimeter metre of poetry that has three iambic (two-syllable) units per line

imagery pictures that words create in your mind as you are reading

immortal never dying

Industrial Revolution period beginning in the late 18th century, in which technology and machinery began to be widely used to make products

introspective being deeply aware of one's own thoughts and feelings

irony literary device in which the writer describes something that is the opposite of its usual or expected meaning

jubilee grand celebration to mark the anniversary of an important event

meditative having an atmosphere that promotes deep thought

metaphor literary device that draws a comparison between two seemingly unrelated things

metre regular pattern of stressed and unstressed syllables in a line of poetry, creating the rhythm of the verse

microcosm world existing in a very small space, but which reflects the wider world

mured imprisoned, or literally built into a wall

mutable changeable, or likely to change

narrative story that follows a sequence of events

neologism either an existing word that has been given a new meaning, or a new word made up to serve a writer's purpose

personification when human characteristics or behaviour are applied to non-human things

plashless word made up by Emily Dickinson to describe how butterflies "swim" through the air

pseudonym made-up name sometimes used by authors to conceal their true identity

Pulitzer Prize annual American award for excellence in journalism, literature, or music

reclusive avoiding company and choosing to live removed from the outside world

rhetorical questions questions that do not require an answer and which are only intended to stimulate thought

rhythm repeated sound you can hear in spoken poetry, created by patterns of stressed and unstressed syllables

Romantic person who followed the Romantic movement, which began in the late 18th century and which believed that art and writing should be about the free expression of thoughts and ideas

rushes tall, grass-like plants that grow in marshy areas

seedling young plant that is grown from a seed rather than a cutting

sequoia huge evergreen tree with red bark, native to California; the same younger (and therefore much smaller) tree grows in the UK, where it is known as the Wellingtonia

stanza group of related lines in a poem, which may have a particular pattern

stressed given emphasis (the opposite is "unstressed")

structure form or shape of a poem; for example, the length of the lines, and whether the poem is split into stanzas and, if so, how long they are

symbolism the expression of ideas or meanings through symbols, rather than explaining them directly

symmetry having two halves that mirror each other, or having equal and balanced proportions

theme key idea that the poet wants the reader to think about

transcendentalist someone who believes that truth and goodness come from within a person, through personal thought and spirituality, rather than through institutions or society

tumultuous noisy and confused

Find out more

Books

Movin': Teen Poets Take Voice, Dave Johnson (ed.) (Orchard Books, 2000)
An anthology of poetry by children, written for workshops at the New York Public Library. The poems cover real-life issues and topics that affect teens.

Painless Poetry, Mary Elizabeth (Barron's Educational Services, 2011)
A good introduction to reading, analysing, and writing poetry. This book will help you overcome your fear of poetry through fun activities, brain teasers, and tips for making poetry fun.

Seeing the Blue Between: Advice and Inspiration for Young Poets, Paul Janeczko (Candlewick, 2002)
A wealth of advice to young writers from 32 experienced poets. Contains letters and poems from these best-loved poets from around the world.

Teen Sunshine Reflections: Words for the Heart and Soul, June Cotner (ed.) (Harper Trophy, 2002)
An anthology of short poems for teens, specifically about spiritual issues, including poems by inspiring figures such as the Dalai Lama, Mahatma Gandhi, Mother Theresa, and e.e. cummings.

The Body Eclectic: An Anthology of Poems, Patrice Vecchione (ed.) (Henry Holt Co., 2002)
A diverse collection of poetry about the human body, including parts that are frequently ignored or misunderstood.

Poetry for Young People: Langston Hughes, David Roessel and Arnold Rampersad (Sterling Children's Books, 2013)
The Poetry for Young People series explores the works of notable poets, which includes the poems of Langston Hughes, an important African American author who wrote about his thoughts and experiences in the early 20th century.

Websites

**www.bbc.co.uk/schools/gcsebitesize/english_literature/
poetryplace**
**www.bbc.co.uk/schools/gcsebitesize/english_literature/
poetryconflict**
The BBC GCSE Bitesize website has selections of poems that are linked
by different themes. Try the links above for the themes of place and
conflict, then search for other themes.

www.poetry4kids.com/rhymes
For a rhyming dictionary where you can type in a word and ask for a
list of words that contain the same sound.

www.poetryarchive.org/poetryarchive/home.do
The Poetry Archive is continually building a huge online library of
poetry selected by a panel of writers and critics. Poems can be searched
by poet name, title, theme, and form.

www.poetryfoundation.org
The Poetry Foundation is dedicated to stimulating interest in poetry
and keeping it alive in modern culture. The website contains extensive
biographies of important poets, along with examples of their work.

Acknowledgements
We would like to thank the following for permission to reproduce photographs:

Corbis pp. 28 29 (Bettmann), 37 (Bettmann), 38–39 (Scott Stulberg),
43 (Lynn Goldsmith), 47l (Wpehlemann), 47r (Marcouliana); Dreamstime
pp. 14–15 (Jaweljawel), 21 (Jorgeantonio), 34–35 (Rcphoto), 40 (Perstralinger),
41 (Valbunny), 52 (Fergs25); Getty Images pp. 8 (British Library/Robana),
11 (Science & Society Picture Library), 18 (Time & Life Pictures); Library of
Congress pp. 24, 31; Shutterstock cover (Krivosheev Vitaly) pp. 5 (Jaroslaw
Grudzinski), 6 (Rob Hainer), 12 (Ludmila Yilmaz), 16–17 (Julie Lubick), 20
(Henrik Larsson), 23 (Eric Isselee), 27 (Fotokostic), 30–31 (Jaroslaw Grudzinski),
36 (Glamorous Images), 42 (kawhia), 44–45 (Mr. Green), 46 (Triff), 48 (Lance
O. Brown), 51 (Allen Furmanski), 53 (Richard Whitcombe), 54 55 (Fillip Fuxa),
56–57 (iPhotos); SuperStock pp. 13 (Fine Art Images), 25 (Susan E. Pease/age
fotostock); Wikipedia pp. 19, 49 (Brett Weinstein).

Index